3849

SOL
CORNET/TRUMPET

CONCERT PIECES

for

TRUMPET

and

CONCERT BAND

Music Minus One

SUGGESTIONS FOR USING THIS MMO EDITION

WE HAVE TRIED to create a product that will provide you an easy way to learn and perform these compositions with a complete accompaniment in the comfort of your own home. Because it involves a fixed accompaniment performance, there is an inherent lack of flexibility in tempo. The following MMO features and techniques will reduce these inflexibilities and help you maximize the effectiveness of the MMO practice and performance system:

Where the soloist begins a piece or movement *solo*, we have provided subtle introductory taps, inserted at the actual tempo before the soloist's entrance.

Chapter stops on your CD are conveniently located throughout the piece at the beginnings of practice sections, and are cross-referenced in the score. This should help you quickly find a desired place in the music as you learn the piece.

Chapter stops have also been placed at orchestra entrances (after cadenzas, for example) so that, with the help of a second person, it is possible to perform a seamless version of the concerto alongside your MMO CD accompaniment. While we have allotted what is generally considered an average amount of time for a cadenza, each performer will have a different interpretation and observe individual tempi. Your personal rendition may preclude a perfect "fit" within the space provided.

Therefore, by having a second person press the pause ❙❙ button on your CD player after the start of each cadenza, followed by the next track ▶▶❙ button, your CD will be cued to the orchestra's re-entry. When you as soloist are at the end of the cadenza or other solo passage, the second person can press the play ▶ (or pause ❙❙ button) on the CD remote to allow a synchronized orchestra re-entry.

We have observed generally accepted tempi, but some may wish to perform at a different tempo, or to slow down or speed up the accompaniment for practice purposes. We have provided a special version of the accompaniment which has been slowed by approximately 20 percent, which you can use while you are learning and practicing each piece. For even more flexibility, you can purchase from MMO specialized CD players & recorders which allow variable speed while maintaining proper pitch. This is an indispensable tool for the serious musician and you may wish to look into purchasing this useful piece of equipment for full enjoyment of all your MMO editions.

We want to provide you with the most useful practice and performance accompaniments possible. If you have any suggestions for improving the MMO system, please feel free to contact us. You can reach us by e-mail at *mmogroup@musicminusonecom*.

3849

CONTENTS

TECHNICAL CREDITS

Recorded 10-12 May 2003, National Philharmonie of Kiev, Ukraine
Richard Carson Steuart, soloist
State Wind-Orchestra of the Ukraine
Alexi Roschak, Conductor
Engineer: Boris Archimovich
Mastered at Marell Studios, Würzburg, Germany
Mastering Engineer: Alexander Klebel
Audio Producer: Richard Carson Steuart

ISBN 1-59615-102-1

Herbert L. Clarke's *Stars in a Velvety Sky*

Conductor, Composer and world famous Cornet-soloist Herbert Lincoln Clarke was born in the small town of Woburn, Massachusetts (near Boston) on 12 September 1867, into a traditional musical family, his father being Dr. W. Horatio Clarke, a famous Organist and composer in his own right.

The young Herbert Clarke revealed himself from a very early age to have an exceptional aptitude for music, and he began his studies first on the violin and then the viola. At age fourteen he started to study the cornet, by far the most popular of all solo brass instruments at that time.

Clarke is best remembered as a virtuoso soloist in the Concert Band medium, having toured the world with the most famous bands of his time, such as those of Victor Herbert, P.S. Gilmore and John Philip Sousa, acting simultaneously as 1st Solo Cornet and featured Soloist, as was the tradition in bands at that time. But he also enjoyed great success in the symphonic medium. He performed in numerous symphony orchestras, including the orchestra of the Metropolitan Grand Opera of New York City, under world-famous conductors of that time such as Engelbert Humperdinck, Adolf Neuendorff and Enrico Bevignani.

Later, Clarke gained an international reputation as conductor of many a fine military concert band, including the Rhode Island Light Infantry Band, the Naval Brigade Band of Massachusetts and during his term as "Bandmaster" of the Second Regiment Military Band of Rhode Island Clarke received his commission as officer.

Later in his career he led a number of privately funded ensembles, including factory bands such as the then-famous "Huntsville Leather Company" band of Huntsville Ontario, Canada and "Reeves' American Band" at Providence, Rhode Island.

Clarke was one of the most successful solo cornetists and teachers of his time in the U.S. He unfortunately regarded "Jaz"—as he wrote the musical term—to be the work of "the devil" and believed too that the trumpet was little more than a passing fad, a solo brass instrument he felt would certainly never reach the popularity and artistic level of the traditional cornet. Despite his short-sightedness in these regards, Clarke was certainly a highly sought-after and widely respected teacher, and it is reported that he was even visited for lessons by such artists of the following generation as the phenomenally virtuoso trumpeter Rafael Méndez.

Clarke wrote a series of what are widely considered to be excellent technical and "characteristic" study books aimed at mastering technical performance on the cornet. These are certainly to be recommended to this day for use by any and all serious students of not only the trumpet and cornet, but for the mastery of performance on virtually all brass instruments.

———

Clarke of course wrote a number of fine original and descriptive virtuoso solos for cornet with concert band accompaniment, including the STARS IN A VELVETY SKY (FANTASY BRILLIANT) presented on this album. This specific work was written and dedicated to none less than John Philip Sousa himself, as a personal congratulations from Clarke to the world-famous Conductor and "March King." The work premiered on the special occasion of the announcement of Sousa's commission as officer in the U.S. Army.

It is a charmingly traditional American "Romantic" fantasy with several attractive "modern melodies" typical of that time. The work has an unpretentiously light musical character, clearly reflecting the positive and pleasantly naïve musical tastes of pre-First World-War America.

The form of this nostalgic work, with its finger-technical *bravura* section (reminiscent of Nikolai Rimsky-Korsakov's *Flight of the Bumble Bee*), its beautifully lyrical *Grazioso* (graceful) section and before the final cadenza and melodic recapitulation, an obligatory "triple tonguing" section marked *Simplice*, is typical of the admittedly somewhat superficial but highly entertaining works written for the virtuoso cornet—soloists of the late Romantic era, such as J.B. Arban, Jules Levy, Èmile Trognèe, Vassily Brandt and Oskar Böhme.

This work has a very special meaning for me personally, since I can most vividly remember enjoying my first performance of it for my television debut at the age of 10, and despite my early age and my understandably obvious lack of musical experience at that time, I clearly remember having no trouble grasping the work's uncomplicated and joyful musical message. I sincerely hope the listener and performer of this work will also enjoy listening to my interpretation of the work and playing it together with the prepared MMO band accompaniment on this CD.

Arban's *Variations on Carnival of Venice*

WORLD-RENOWNED CORNET SOLOIST JEAN BAPTIST LAU-
RENT ARBAN was born in Lyon, France on February 28,
1825. After his studies with F. G. A. Dauverné at the
Paris Conservatory, graduating with a "First Prize" (top
of his class and with "First Class Honors") at 20 years
of age, he began his career as a member of the French
Navy in the Music Corps on the ship "La Belle Poule"
under the famous military musical director Paulus who
later became the *Directeur de la Garde a Paris* during
the reign of Napoleon II. It was a combination of Arban's
brilliant virtuosity on the cornet and his genius as an
exceptional musical personality that were undoubtedly
responsible for his phenomenal success as a soloist. He
performed hundreds of concerts each year for the both
the general public as well as "private" concerts for several of the crowned heads of Europe. Arban is reported
to have received numerous honors from the European
Aristocracy for his extraordinary performance and was
named officer of the French *Académie,* Knight of the
"Order of Leopold" of Belgium, of "Isabella the Catho-
lic," of "Christ of Portugal," and even personally received
the "Cross of Russia" from Tsar Alexander III, who hap-
pened to be an avid "hobby" cornetist of quite consider-
able achievement. Alexander III often performed on the
high brass instruments up to the time he became Tsar,
owning 2 "quartets" of very fine hand-made cornets in
"horn-form" with rotary valves. (I had the great pleasure
of playing one of these instruments during the European
Trumpet Guild conference in 2001, when it was brought
from a private St. Petersburg Museum to be displayed in
the famous Trumpet Museum in Bad Säckingen, Germany.)

A few words should be spoken about the cornet. The
French term "cornet" actually means a "small horn"
(*cor* being the French term for horn and *corno* the Ital-
ian). The true full French name is actually *Cornet á
(avec) piston*, literally meaning "small horn with (piston-
)valves."

The primary difference between trumpet and cornet
is the relationship between conical and cylindrical tubing
(regardless of the kind of valves; rotary, piston or oth-
erwise added to it). Most important are: the cup-shape
of the mouthpiece; the conical development of the lead
pipe; the relationship between the conical and cylindrical parts of the middle section of the instrument; and,
finally, the size and shape of the bell. These combined
factors are all very important in the production of the
characteristically dark and warm tone of the cornet, as
opposed to the more brilliant and aggressive-sounding
trumpet.

Unfortunately many trumpeters mistakenly
attempted to play the cornet as if it where a trumpet,
blowing much too loudly and often too high on the cornet,
as if they where playing a jazz trumpet of the 1920s,
resorting to the use of mouthpieces that have much too
flat a cup and too small a bore size, thus making the
cornet produce a thin and harsh tone. If they would at
least use a proper V-cup cornet mouthpiece they would
easily produce the extraordinarily warm, rich and very
beautiful sound associated with the cornet of the 19th
century.

Richard Stegmann, my predecessor at the Bavar-
ian State Conservatory of Music in Würzburg, Germany,
was—aside from being a fine orchestral trumpeter performing on the German "rotary-valve" trumpet and a
long time member of the Berlin Philharmonic—a true
virtuoso on the Cornet. In Germany, this instrument is
to this day often referred to as simply a "Piston," and
this even when it had rotary valves! Stegmann pre-
ferred, however, to perform on the "French" cornet (with
piston or "Perinett" valves) instead of rotary valves. The
German rotary-valve version called the Kornett was very
popular up to Second World War and, though seldom
played today, was also an excellent solo instrument, pro-
ducing just as beautiful, full and dark a tone quality as
the French models at that time. (It should be noted that
even the great Russian solo trumpeter, Timofei Dok-
shitzer, started his career in the Russian Military on
such a "German" or "rotary-valve" Kornett, advancing
to one of the greatest solo trumpeters of all time).

Arban was quite undoubtedly one of most, if not
the most, important artistic personality in advancing
the cornet (and consequently the trumpet) to its still-
high status as one of the most popular of all musical
instruments. Arban's world famous "Method for the
Cornet," written for perfecting the technical and musical performance on the instrument was, when presented
to the Commission of the Paris Conservatory in the late
1860s, unanimously acclaimed, accredited and recommended for use in that fabled institution "without res-
ervation."

This illustrious commission that judged Arban's
new "method" included such distinguished musicians as
Meyerbeer, Auber and even Arban's earlier teacher, the
famous trumpeter Dauverné.

After a time as professor of the Saxhorn at the
French Military School (from 1857), Arban was elected
professor of the Paris Conservatory in 1869. However,
due to his heavy schedule as a touring concert soloist, Arban held this position only sporadically until 1880, when
he finally returned to teach steadily at the Conservatory
until his death in 1889.

Arban's "Cornet Method" is without a doubt the most
important work written for instruction on high brass

instruments of its time and, in fact, must certainly be regarded as such today. It is in any case Arban's legacy to generations of aspiring artists of the brass instrument, and is the embodiment of this great musician's long experience as both an exceptionally brilliant cornet soloist and excellent teacher. It is certainly the most important book a trumpeter can own for developing his or her technical abilities.

The *Fantaisié and Variations* on the famous *Carnival of Venice* remains to this day an icon in the cornetist or trumpeter's repertoire, and still "sorts the men out from boys" as my father would say, with regards to the virtuosity, both in terms of technical aspects and of true musical expression on the instrument. Unfortunately Arban's "Carnival" is, as are many fine original Romantic cornet-solos with theme and variations, often regarded today as little more than trite "circus number" by uneducated "trumpet jocks" who prefer to screech out high notes rather than learn to make descriptive sensitive music with a depth of emotion on the trumpet or cornet.

I'm sure if the reader is an aspiring soloist himself he has long since understood this mistake of judgment, and dismissed such nonsense as what it is, namely the confusion of primitive sport with true artistic endeavor. Arban's *Fantaisié and Variations* begin with an Introduction *(Allegretto)* that I have decided to embellish from the very beginning with a series of original "Arban Cadenzas," each of which is printed in his famous *Method for Cornet*. I myself prefer the Carl Fischer edition entitled "Complete Conservatory Method" which, aside from all of the excellent instructional material, also contains Arban's selected duets and his *Art of Phrasing* of "classical and popular melodies"; his *14 Grand Studies*; and his wonderful *Fantaisies and Airs Varies*, twelve virtuoso works, all with variations. This includes the *Fantaisié and Variations* based on the *Carnival of Venice*. There is also a full page of one-line cadenzas in this Edition (on page 15) from which I have drawn almost all of the basic material for the cadenzas presented, and which are re-printed for you in this book.

The beautifully lyrical Introduction soon gives way to the well known "staccato" theme, which I believe is to be played slightly faster than the *Introduction*, but taking care not to hurry the flowing sixteenth-note "sub-variation" which already begins in bar 67. As in every lyrical line a maximum in dynamic contour helps enormously to perform both in both a technically efficient and at the ame time in a musically expressive manner.

The First Variation of the work, beginning at bar 91, should remain in the same tempo as the Theme and in any case not be performed hastily, but rather lightly and crisply, taking care not to rush the "quasi-chromatic" double-tonguing sections starting at Bar 100. The following section (from Bar 107 'til 122) may be played in a *fortissimo/piano* dialog, but the music should certainly not lose its lyrical lightness despite this added technical aspect of dynamic change.

The Second Variation (triple-tonguing) should be a slight bit faster than the previous variation, but again certainly not rushed. Remember that virtuosity is not simply speed as such, but rather "control" and clarity of execution. Musical expression must in any case never suffer at the cost of speed. I suggest in fact that this entire section be practiced very slowly at first making sure each note of the three "tripled-tongued" triplets is produced with equal clarity and fullness of tone. The conscious use of *crescendo* and *diminuendo* in all ascending and descending passages helps greatly to maintain proper air support for every tone produced, especially later when the tempo is gradually increased to its final speed, which I believe should be approximately 62 MM to the dotted quarter-note.

The Third Variation is actually in two parts: first a beautifully melodious *Andante* section and later— beginning at Bar 187—a playful mixed slurring and double tonguing section that can also gradually increase in speed. I have chosen to add a few of my own ideas here, and so to create a "variation within the variation," even adding at the end a few dramatic scales that ascend to a high C and high D respectively (as written for the B-flat cornet).

The Fourth (and Final) Variation is a clever "duet" that the soloist actually performs with himself. It may be played very slowly at first and with a gradual acceleration in tempo, or with a fast but steady tempo from the very beginning. It is necessary to take some time to learn to produce the low notes with tonal quality, however, and it's better not to attempt to perform the variation too quickly.

In the Coda one can certainly play an *accelerando* through to the end of the work, so to give the *Finale* even more excitement (as I have attempted to do on this recording), and/or, if one feels adventuresome, to add a short final cadenza for added musical interest. A sense of good taste should hopefully prevent the performer from trying to play as high and loud a note as possible at the end of this work, a common mistake that has more often than not revealed the performer and his abilities to be little more than ego trip in the form of a circus attraction rather than an artistic musical statement.
I sincerely hope these comments and recordings will be enjoyable and helpful for the listener and that you too will enjoy working with this music as much as I have done.

Willi Liebe's *Der Zugenbrecher (The Tongue Breaker)*
(Realization and arrangement for band by Johannes Brenke)

As was the case with the famous American Cornet virtuoso Herbert L. Clarke, Willi Liebe (1905-1977) was the son of a successful professional musical family. Living in Wuppertal-Elberfeld in the northwestern State of Westfalen in Germany at the end of the Nineteenth Century, Liebe's father was a conductor and trumpeter at the city theater of Elberfeld—the same city where at the age of only twelve years, young Willi made his debut as Cornet soloist in that city's town hall or "Stadthalle." Later, but even before his formal studies had begun, he had already taken a position in the famous Gewandhausorchestra in Leipzig—at the unheard of age fifteen!

After two years in Leipzig, he wisely decided to study the trumpet formally at the State Conservatory in Cologne (Musikhochschule Köln) with Hermann Abenroth as his professor (from 1922 to 1924) and finished his studies in half the "normal time period" and with First-class Honors. At twenty years of age he became the First Solo Trumpeter of the German Opera in Berlin under, among other famous international conductors of that time, the American Bruno Walter. He held that position for the next forty years, until his retirement from orchestral performance.

Due to his extraordinary talents as a virtuoso solo trumpeter in the "popular" music vein of that period, and parallel to his success as orchestral solo trumpeter at the Grand Opera in Berlin, Willi Liebe was soon sought after for his celebrated qualities to entertain the troops, performing numerous concerts throughout Germany during the 1930s and then in the '40s in the "occupied" countries.

Liebe's phenomenal popularity was quickly noticed and exploited by the Nazi regime and he was to become the darling of the German propaganda machine, exempt from "normal" military duties by order of Hitler's diabolical "Propaganda Minister" Dr. Joseph Goebbels. Liebe's association with the Nazi propaganda machine did not prevent him from enjoying great success immediately after the Second World War and well into the late 1960s, performing numerous live radio and television concerts throughout Europe.

Liebe's *Zugenbrecher* is typical of many of his virtuoso solo pieces that he performed throughout German-speaking Europe during his long career. Parallel to his *Liebesgeschichten* (love stories), a *Polka- brilliante* and his *Bravour-Polka*, his repertoire included standard German works such as *Der Alte Dessauer* March, the *Post in Walde*, as well as J.B. Arban's famous version of *Carnival of Venice*. He was in no way averse to giving audiences his interpretations of the less virtuoso, but certainly very effective, world-famous trumpet solo works such as *Il Selenzio* by Nini Rosso.

Willi Liebe was certainly known as a "crowd-pleaser" and ladies man, and his *Zugenbrecher* never failed to astound his audiences with its machine-gun-like rapid triple-tonguing acrobatics.

The works begins with a blustering introduction in the heavy "Prussian Military" tradition: with loud snare drumming, crashing cymbals, and vibrantly ascending woodwind scale passages framed by rhythmic fortissimo brass impulses. This festive introduction quickly becomes subdued, however, and the solo trumpet begins to play a simple, lyrical melody based on tonic triads, ending after only fourteen bars with a short but declamatory cadenza.

The trumpet then announces the first polka theme in a loud fanfare, followed this time by a more aggressive virtuoso cadenza ending after a doubled-tongued two-octave chromatic scale on a fortissimo "high C"(sounding B♭) above the staff. Then, without further ado, the Polka proper starts, with its percussive, arpeggiated melody and *staccato* double and triple-tongued scale passages. After a further short cadenza, this time reaching a high E (sounding D) above the staff, this passage is repeated and the work then modulates into the key of sounding A♭ major for the Trio section of the work.

I believe it is important not to play this "trio"section too quickly since the complicated interval jumps and triple-tonguing "acrobatics" become increasingly more difficult as one approaches the end of the passage at letter H.

The final cadenza begins with a *fermata* followed by an accelerating triple-tongued passage (on middle C on the staff) which, after four bars, reaches its highest tempo and immediately quotes the polka motif once again, proceeding through three double-tongued scale passages to a high C above the staff.

The last doubled-tongued phrase at letter K can just as well be slurred, but the arpeggiated triads that follow the low-C *fermata* should in any case be tongued very clearly.

The final scale passage soaring to the high F above the staff (sounding E♭) can be very tiring for a less-experienced performer may also be effectively performed an octave lower, as is alternatively printed.

Generally speaking, triple-tonguing scale passages with precision on the trumpet is more a question of proper air support and compression rather than tongue movement; but a clear pronunciation of the syllables *Ta Ta Ka* or, better still, *Ti Ti Ki,* is absolutely necessary and must, as with all technical difficulties on the trumpet, be practiced very slowly at first. I suggest accenting the *Ka* or *Ki* syllable to increase the air compression behind the tongue on this less-percussive syllable, assuring a more equal projection of tone on all three syllables when the tempo is increased.

—Richard Carson Steuart

Stars in a Velvety Sky

Solo for Cornet in B♭
with Band Accompaniment

CORNET IN B♭

Herbert L. Clarke

Fantasie and Variations
on
The Carnival of Venice

CORNET IN B♭

J. B. Arban
arr. Roger Jannotta

13

MMO 3849

14

Var.II
Solo

18

Der Zungenbrecher

Willi Liebe
arr. Klaus Dietrich & Johannes Brenke

2

Engraving: Wieslaw Novak

TRUMPET CLASSICS
WITH ORCHESTRA FROM
MUSIC MINUS ONE

Art of the Solo Trumpet
Orchestral Accompaniment ....MMO CD 3807
Peter Piacquadio, trumpet - Stuttgart Festival Orchestra/Emil Kahn: A Baroque extravaganza for trumpet and orchestra with which to pursue your virtuosic endeavors. A beautiful collection which will help you refine your technique with the added dimension of a huge orchestra at your side!
Brandenburg Concerto No. 2 in F major, BWV1047 (I. Allegro; II. Andante; III. Allegro assai); Concerto for Two Trumpets: I. Allegro maestoso; III. Allegro; Sonata for Trumpet and Strings in D major: I. Allegro; III. Allegro; Sonata for Trumpet and Strings in C major (Allegro; Andante; Allegro; Allegretto-Aria); Sonata for Trumpet and Strings in C major (Allegro; Andante; Allegro; Allegretto-Aria); Symphony with Trumpet (I. Allegro; II. Allegro; III. Allegro non troppo)

ARUTIUNIAN Concerto for Trumpet/Cornet & Concert Band; GOEDICKE Concert Etude ....MMO CD 3846
Richard Steuart, trumpet - State Wind Orchestra of the Ukraine/Alexi Roschak: This great 20th-century concerto by Armenian composer Arutiunian has become one of the essential elements for all trumpeters. And virtuoso Richard Steuart demonstrates his approach…you join with the orchestra to work your own magic! DDD

Band Aids *Concert Band Favorites*
with Orchestra...MMO CD 3832
Michael Philip Mossman, trumpet - Stuttgart Festival Orchestra/Emil Kahn: From Bach to Dvorak, this collection of classics arranged presents a unique treat, spanning 200 years of great music, arranged for Trumpet and concert band.
J.S. Bach *Chorale No. 42; Chorale No. 297;* **Beethoven** *Variations on a Theme by Paisiello; Contradanse; The Ruins of Athens, op. 113: Turkish March;* **Brahms** *A Melody Is Drifting;* **Dvorak** *Slavonic Dance;* **D. Gabrielli** *Sacre Symphoniae: Canzon;* **Haydn** *String Quartet in C major, 'Emperor', op. 76, no. 3, HobIII/77: II. Andante;* **Lully** *Minuet;* **Palestrina** *Te Deum Landamus (Mass): Crucifixus;* **Prokofiev** *The Love for Three Oranges: March;* **Smetana** *The Bartered Bride (Prodana Nevesta): Polka;* **Sullivan** *There Lived a King;* **Tchaikovsky** *Romeo and Juliet: Theme;* **Trad. (Hymn)** *Christ the Lord Is Risen Today*

Classics for Trumpet and Concert Band.....................MMO CD 3849
Richard Steuart, trumpet - State Wind Orchestra of the Ukraine/Alexi Roschak: A collection of magical classics for trumpet and concert band; the great Richard Steuart demonstrates, then you walk under the spotlights and make great music! ADD
Liebe *Der Zungenbrecher;* **Arban** *Variations on Carnival of Venice;* **Clarke** *Stars in a Velvety Sky*

First Chair Trumpet Solos
Orchestral Accompaniment ....MMO CD 3806
Peter Piacquadio, trumpet - Stuttgart Festival Orchestra/Emil Kahn: Trumpet solos drawn from every corner of the symphonic repertoire, from Baroque to Late Romantic (Wagner, Bruckner). Every aspect of the orchestral trumpeter's world is explored. Master trumpeter Peter Piacquadio is your guide as you listen to his interpretations of these classic works; then you have the opportunity to practice and perform these with full orchestra in the comfort of your own home!
Brahms *Academic Festival Overture, op. 80: Two excerpts (Allegro; Maestoso);* **Bruckner** *Symphony No. 3 in D minor (Allegro moderato);* **Händel** *The Water Music, HWV348 (Andante Allegro; Allegro maestoso - Hornpipe; Lentemente; Pomposo): The Water Music, HWV348 (Andante Allegro; Allegro maestoso - Hornpipe; Lentemente; Pomposo);* **Mendelssohn** *Calm Sea and Prosperous Voyage, op. 27;* **Suppé** *Overture to Light Cavalry;* **Wagner** *Rienzi, der Letzte der Tribunen, WWV49: Overture*

Opera Arias for Trumpet and Orchestra, vol. I.......MMO CD 3847
Richard Steuart - Plovdiv Philharmonic Orchestra; Sofia National Opera/Nayden Todorov: Join European trumpet sensation Richard Steuart playing the great operatic aria themes with a thrilling full orchestra! Then it's your turn to join the group with conductor Nayden Todorov at the helm! DDD
Donizetti *L'Elisir d'Amore - Act II: 'Una furtiva lagrima' (Nemorino); Lucia di Lammermoor - Act III: '...Fra poco a me ricovero' (Edgardo);* **Leoncavallo** *I Pagliacci - Act I: 'Recitar!...Vesti la giubba' (Canio/Pagliaccio);* **Massenet** *Werther - Act III: 'Pourquoi me réveiller?' (Werther);* **Puccini** *La Bohème - Act I: 'Mi chiamano Mimi' (Mimi); Act II: 'Quando m'en vo' soletta la via' (Musetta);* **Gianni Schicchi:** *'O mio babbino caro' (Lauretta); La Rondine - Act I: 'Chi il bel sogno di Doretta' (Magda); Turandot - Act III: 'Nessun dorma' (Calaf);*

Opera Arias for Trumpet and Orchestra, vol. II......MMO CD 3848
Richard Steuart - Plovdiv Philharmonic Orchestra; Sofia National Opera/Nayden Todorov: Richard Steuart brings you a second album of opera classics arranged for trumpet and orchestra! Then you step in to blow your horn with a full ensemble! DDD
Bizet *Carmen - Act I: 'L'amour est un oiseau rebelle' (La Habanera) (Carmen); di Capua* *'O Sole Mio!;* **Lehár** *Die Lustige Witwe (The Merry Widow): 'Vilja'; Act I: 'O Vaterland' (Danilo) (highlights); Act III: 'Lippen schweigen' (Duett: Hanna, Danilo);* **Schubert** *Ellens Gesang III: 'Ave Maria', op. 52, no. 6;* **J. Strauss, Jr.** *Die Fledermaus - Act II: Csárdás; 7. Couplets ('Ich lade gern mir Gäste ein');* **Verdi** *Rigoletto - Act III: 'La donna è mobile' (Duca);*

Three Trumpet Concerti - HAYDN E-flat major, HobVIIe:1; TELEMANN D major; FASCH D major.................MMO CD 3801
Brian Rood, trumpet - Stuttgart Festival Orchestra/Emil Kahn: Three major trumpet concerti on one disc, complete with full orchestral accompaniment. MMO's most popular trumpet album. Digitally remastered for brilliant sound! *2 CD Set* ADD
Trumpet Concerto in D major; Trumpet Concerto in E-flat major, HobVIIe/1; Trumpet Concerto in D major

Popular Concert Favorites for Trumpet
with Orchestra ....MMO CD 3831
Michael Philip Mossman, trumpet - Stuttgart Festival Orchestra/Emil Kahn: Here is a collection of concert pieces for trumpet and orchestra that demonstrate the instrument's capabilities admirably. Of easy to intermediate difficulty, these selections with full orchestral background provide the early-level trumpeter a thrilling theatre in which to practice and perform. Sensitive arrangements to be treasured by beginner and professional alike.
J.S. Bach *Sarabande;* **Bizet** *Carmen: Toreador Song;* **Chopin** *Prelude, op. 28, no. 7;* **Dittersdorf** *Tournament of Temperaments (The Melancholic, The Humble, The Gentle);* **MacDowell** *To a Wild Rose;* **Mendelssohn** *Solemn March;* **Schubert** *Moment Musical, op. 94, D780, no. 3;* **Schumann** *Kinderszenen, op. 15: 7. Träumerei;* **Verdi** *Aïda: Triumphal March*

SOUSA Marches plus BEETHOVEN, BERLIOZ,
STRAUSS ....MMO CD 3810
Peter Piacquadio, trumpet - Stuttgart Festival Orchestra/Emil Kahn: This energetic and thrilling collection of marches for trumpet by the great John Philip Sousa is complemented by other march classics by such greats as Beethoven, Berlioz and more. It is a thrilling experience to play these classics with a huge orchestral band!
Beethoven *Military March;* **Berlioz** *Rakoczy March;* **Schrammel** *Vienna Forever;* **Sousa** *The Washington Post; The Stars & Stripes Forever; The Liberty Bell; Semper Fidelis; The 'El Capitan' March; The Gladiator March;* **J. Strauss, Jr.** *The Radetzky March*

DDD digital stereo recording   ADD fully digitally remastered stereo analogue
recording for the ultimate in sonic fidelity

FOR OUR FULL TRUMPET CATALOGUE
visit us on the web at
www.musicminusone.com

MUSIC MINUS ONE
50 Executive Boulevard • Elmsford, New York 10523-1325
800-669-7464 (U.S.)/914-592-1188 (International)

www.musicminusone.com